NATURE CLOSE-UP

JUNIORS

Forest Floor

TEXT BY ELAINE PASCOE

PHOTOGRAPHS BY DWIGHT KUHN

BLACKBIRCH PRESS

An imprint of Thomson Gale, a part of The Thomson Corporation

THOMSON
™
GALE

Detroit • New York • San Francisco • San Diego • New Haven, Conn. • Waterville, Maine • London • Munich

THOMSON

GALE

For more information, contact
Blackbirch Press.
27500 Drake Rd.
Farmington Hills, MI 48331-3535
Or you can visit our Internet site at http://www.gale.com

Photo Credits: All pages © Dwight R. Kuhn Photography

LIBRARY OF CONGRESS CATALOGING-IN-PUBLICATION DATA

Pascoe, Elaine.
Forest Floor / text by Elaine Pascoe ; photographs by Dwight Kuhn.
  p. cm. — (Nature close-up junior)
 Includes bibliographical references and index.
 ISBN 1-4103-0314-4 (hardcover : alk. paper)

Printed in China
10 9 8 7 6 5 4 3 2 1

Contents

Read this first:

Have fun when you explore the forest floor, but be smart. Take an adult with you. Walk carefully. Don't bother the animals that you see—just enjoy them.

Take a walk in a forest. Trees are all around you. Their fallen leaves and branches cover the ground. You can hear your footsteps crunching in the leaves. If you stop to look and listen, you will see and hear much more.

The forest floor is full of living things. It is a great home, or **habitat,** for plants and animals. The plants and animals depend on each other. Together, they form a community.

Some of the animals that live here are very small. Some are very shy. You will have to look closely to see them.

The forest floor is home to many plants and animals.

Leaf Litter

Leaves fall from the trees. They pile up in layers on the forest floor. The leaves are dead. But they have a big role in the life of the forest.

Fallen leaves pile up on the forest floor. They rot and make the soil rich.

The leaves slowly rot as they lie on the ground. They crumble away, forming new soil. The new soil is rich in **nutrients** that plants need.

Trees and other plants take in these nutrients through their roots. They use the nutrients to grow and put out new leaves. Then those leaves die and fall to the ground. They rot and put nutrients back in the soil. The cycle begins again.

The forest soil is a great place for new plants to grow. In spring, ferns push up through the leaf litter. Seeds **sprout.** A tiny oak begins to grow from an acorn that fell to the ground last fall. After many years of growth, the oak will be a tall forest tree.

A new oak sprouts from an acorn. Its roots grow down into the soil.

Mushrooms

Look closely at the leaf litter. You may see mushrooms growing there. Mushrooms are not plants. They belong to the fungus family. Some mushrooms are poisonous, so don't eat any that you find.

A mushroom is only part of a fungus. Under the leaf litter, the fungus spreads a net of tiny threads. The threads soak up nutrients from the rotting leaves.

Mushrooms pop up above the leaf litter. They grow in many shapes and colors. Puffball mushrooms look like little balls. Cap mushrooms look like little umbrellas. Tiny grains called spores are packed under the cap, in slits called **gills**. The spores are like seeds. Each can grow into a new fungus.

Top: Cap mushrooms look like little umbrellas. *Bottom:* A puffball mushroom sends out a puff of tiny spores.

Mushroom Spore Print

Cap mushrooms have gills under their caps. But each kind of mushroom has its own gill pattern. A spore print is like a fungus fingerprint. It shows the mushroom's gill pattern.

What to do:
- Pick a mushroom with an open cap. You should be able to see the gills.
- Break off the stem just under the cap.
- Put the cap on the paper, gill side down.
- Cover the cap with a bowl or glass.
- Leave the mushroom on the paper overnight. Be careful not to move it.
- In the morning, lift the bowl. Carefully remove the mushroom.

You will see a pattern on the paper. It is made of spores that fell out of the mushroom. The spores will easily blow away, so don't breathe on them.

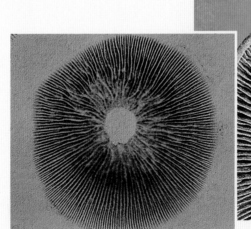

Snails, Slugs, and Slimy Worms

Use a stick to push aside some damp leaves. You may see earthworms wiggling in the leaf litter. You may find snails or slugs. These little animals hide in damp places during the day.

Earthworms, snails, and slugs have soft bodies that can dry out easily. They are covered with slimy **mucus.** The mucus helps keep them from drying out.

Earthworms crawl on the forest floor. They eat bits of dead leaves.

Earthworms are good for the forest. They eat bits of fallen leaves and other dead matter. They break down these bits. Then they cast out wastes. Their wastes make rich soil that helps plants grow.

Earthworms help the forest in other ways. They tunnel down into the ground. This loosens the soil and helps air and water reach plant roots.

Snails and slugs leave silvery trails of slime as they creep along. A snail carries its house—a hard shell—on its back. If danger threatens, the snail pulls its body inside the shell. Slugs are related to snails, but they have no shells.

Snails and slugs eat plants and dead matter that they find on the forest floor. Like earthworms, they are part of the forest cleanup crew.

A snail carries its shell as it creeps over a leaf.

Snails Up Close

If you find a snail in the woods, you can carry it home in a jar for a closer look. When you are done watching it, take it back where you found it. You can also buy live snails at a pet store or through the mail. See page 24 for some sources. Snails that you buy should not be let go in the wild.

See page 24 for some sources.

What You Need:
- Wide-mouth jar or other clear container
- Damp soil, leaf litter, and pieces of bark or sticks
- Water in a spray bottle
- Mesh
- Rubber band
- Lettuce and other snail food

Making a snail home:
- Put some damp soil and leaf litter in the bottom of the jar. Add a few sticks or pieces of bark for snails to hide under.
- Put in the snails. Then cover the jar with the mesh and a rubber band.

Caring for snails:
- Add food each evening. Snails like lettuce, spinach, carrots, fruits, and mushrooms. Give them water by spraying it on their food. Take out uneaten food and snail droppings.
- Keep the snail home in a cool, shady place. Mist the soil lightly with water to keep it slightly damp, but not soggy.

- If you take snails out of their home, keep them damp. Put them on damp paper towels. Mist them with water.

Watching snails:

- Watch your snails in their jar. How do they move? Where does the slime come from?
- Take a snail from the jar. Put it on a damp paper towel. What does it do when you touch it? When you put a stick in its path? How far does it go in a minute?

A cricket's big hind legs are built for hopping.

Chirpers and Spinners

Lots of insects live on the forest floor. How can you tell if something is an insect? Count the legs! Insects have six legs.

Some insects are easier to hear than to see. During the day, crickets hide in cool, dark places. At night they come out. You may hear them chirping. Crickets rub their wings together to make their music. It's as if the crickets were playing little fiddles.

Many insects spend only part of their lives on the forest floor. A luna moth begins its life in a tree. It hatches from an egg as a green caterpillar. The caterpillar crawls around in the tree, eating leaves. It grows fast. After a few weeks, it begins to spin a silky thread. It winds the thread around its body, making a **cocoon.** It pulls a leaf into its cocoon, making a papery wrap of silk and leaves.

The cocoon falls to the ground. It lies on the forest floor among the leaves. Inside, the insect slowly changes into an adult moth. Finally it crawls out and spreads its new wings. The wings are soft and wrinkled at first. But they soon dry and stiffen. Then the moth flies away.

Below: A luna moth caterpillar. *Right, inset:* A cocoon on the ground. *Right:* An adult luna moth.

A millipede crawls along a piece of rotting wood.

A female wolf spider carries her eggs in a white silk sac.

Lots of Legs

Animals besides insects live on the forest floor. Use a stick to turn over a stone or log. You may find centipedes or millipedes. Centipedes bite, so do not pick them up. Most centipedes have thirty legs. Some millipedes have more than three hundred legs!

Wood lice also hide under stones and logs. Their hard shells look like little suits of armor. They eat rotting leaves and other dead material. Two main kinds of wood lice are sow bugs and pill bugs. When a pill bug is scared, it curls up in a tight little ball. It looks like a pill.

Spiders have eight legs. They catch and eat insects. Some kinds of spiders catch **prey** in webs. The wolf spider hunts its prey. This hairy spider looks scary. But it is not poisonous.

Wood Lice Up Close

You can keep wood lice for a short time and watch them.

What to do:

- Put some damp soil in your jar. Add bark or a stone for the animals to hide under.
- Collect a few wood lice. Pick them up gently with a spoon or tweezers. Put them in the jar.
- Cover the jar. Use plastic wrap with air holes and a rubber band.
- Keep the jar in a cool, shady place. Keep the soil slightly damp by misting with water.
- Feed wood lice bits of moist lettuce, apple, and potato. Add fresh food every day, and take out old food.

Watching wood lice:

- Use a hand lens to study the wood lice. How many legs do they have? Can you find their eyes?
- Watch the animals. Where do they spend most of their time? What do they do if you touch them?

When you are done, put the wood lice back where you found them.

What You Need:
- Jar or plastic container
- Vented plastic wrap
- Rubber band
- Damp soil and a piece of bark or a stone
- Lettuce and other food
- Water in a spray bottle

Toads and Turtles

A toad's skin is brown and bumpy. The toad looks just like a dead leaf—until it hops! The toad spends the day hiding among the leaves. At night it hunts for insects. When an insect comes near, the toad flicks out its long, sticky tongue and grabs its meal.

Toads and frogs are close relatives. They belong to a group of animals called **amphibians.** They begin their lives in water, as tadpoles. Tadpoles breathe water through **gills**, like fish. But their bodies slowly change. They grow legs. They develop lungs, to breathe air. As adults they live on land.

Box turtles are **reptiles.** They spend a lot of time buried in the leaf litter. But they come out to feed on mushrooms, earthworms, slugs, and insects. If a box turtle is afraid, it pulls its head and legs into its shell. It closes the shell tight and waits until the danger is gone.

A toad blends in with the dead leaves of its forest home.

16

Box turtles can live to be 120 years old. But they are not as common as they once were. One reason is that people have taken them as pets. If you see one, leave it where it is. Do not take it from the wild.

The hard shell of this box turtle is like a suit of armor.

A tiny white-footed mouse looks for food on the forest floor.

Furry Forest Dwellers

A white-footed mouse scurries around the forest floor looking for seeds, nuts, and other things to eat. It can stuff its cheeks with seeds and carry them back to its nest. The nest may be among the leaves or under a log.

Mice are **mammals.** They have fur. They give birth to live young. And the young feed on their mother's milk. A female white-footed mouse may have several litters of pups each year.

There are lots of mice in the forest. But you may not see them. They hide during the day and come out at night. They must be careful. Many **predators** hunt for mice. Owls and snakes eat mice. So do weasels.

The short-tailed weasel is only about 1 foot (30 cm) long. But it is a fierce hunter. It can eat several mice a day. It can kill rabbits and other animals, too.

Weasels and other predators are important to the forest. They keep the number of mice in check. If there were no predators, mice might eat all the seeds. Then new plants would not grow. Predators help keep the forest community in balance.

Right: The short-tailed weasel hunts for mice and other small forest animals.

19

What Lives in the Forest Floor?

Many animals of the forest floor are small and hard to find. They live in the leaf litter and in the top layer of soil, just under the leaves. Here is an activity that will help you find out what little animals are in a patch of forest floor.

What to do:

- Push aside the leaf litter. Dig a hole deep enough to hold your container.
- Bury the container with the top edge at ground level. Put the wood over it. Put sticks or stones under each end of the board, so there is a space between the wood and the edge of the container.

What You Need:
- Plastic container with steep sides
- Trowel or shovel
- Wood to cover the container
- Hand lens

- Leave the container buried overnight. Go back the next day to see if any little animals have fallen into your trap.
- Use a hand lens to look at the animals. Count their legs. See if you can figure out what they are. Use the pictures in this book or an insect field guide.
- Lift the container out of the ground. Turn it over and shake out the animals to let them go. If you want, bury the container again to see what else you can catch.

Words to Know

amphibians: animals that spend part of their lives in water and part on land.

cocoon: a silk wrapping in which a caterpillar changes into a moth.

gills: in mushrooms, tiny slits that hold spores. In animals, body parts for taking oxygen from water, or breathing water.

habitat: the place where a plant or animal naturally lives.

mammals: animals that have fur, give birth to live young, and nurse their young with milk.

mucus: a slimy substance made by glands in the body.

nutrients: substances that a plant or animal needs to live.

predators: animals that kill and eat other animals.

prey: animals that are hunted by predators

reptiles: cold-blooded, air-breathing animals with backbones and scales or hard plates.

sprout: begin to grow.

For More Information

Books

Nic Bishop, *Forest Explorer: A Life-Sized Field Guide.* New York: Scholastic, 2004.

Diane L. Burns, *Frogs, Toads, and Turtles.* Minnetonka, MN: NorthWord Press, 1997.

Allan Fowler, *Of Mice and Rats.* Danbury, CT: Children's Press, 1999.

Gallimard Jeunesse, *Turtles and Snails.* New York: Cartwheel Books, August 1998

Carolyn B. Otto, *Spiders.* New York: Scholastic, 2002.

Matthew Reinhart, *Young Naturalist's Handbook: Insect-lo-pedia.* New York: Hyperion, 2003.

Web Sites

Just for Kids (www.fs.fed.us/kids).
Smokey Bear and Woodsy Owl guide kids through this site from the U.S. Forest Service.

Kidzone (www.nwf.org/kids).
This site from the National Wildlife Federation has information on wildlife and habitats.

Sources

Sources for snails:

Carolina Biological Supply Company
2700 York Rd.
Burlington, NC 27215
(800) 334-5551
www.carosci.com

Connecticut Valley Biological Supply
82 Valley Rd., PO Box 326
Southampton, MA 01073
(800) 628-7748
www.ctvalleybio.com

Index